THE GETTYSBURG BATTLEFIELD TOUR BOOK

by

Dr. Michael R. McGough, D.Ed.

Maj. Gen. George G. Meade
USA

General Robert E. Lee
CSA

Purpose

This guide will enable visitors to the Gettysburg National Military Park and Cemetery to tour these areas on their own. The text is keyed to a sixteen stop tour route outlined on the back cover. Carefully following the tour route with the aid of this book will offer a general understanding and appreciation of the Battle of Gettysburg, the area in which it took place, and its legacy. For a more detailed interpretation, consult the SUGGESTED READING LIST and/or obtain the services of a Licensed Battlefield Guide through the National Park Service.

Directions for use

Information and official park folders outlining the tour route can be obtained free from the Visitor Center of the Gettysburg National Military Park, located on Business Route 15 South, Steinwehr Avenue. Before you begin your tour, we suggest you read SUMMARY OF THE CAMPAIGN in this guide. At a relaxed pace, you should be able to complete the entire tour route in two to three hours. As you enjoy the park, please observe these rules:

- Park only in designated areas.

- Lock your vehicle when you leave it unattended.

- Limit your use of bicycle, motorcycle, or moped to designated roadways, obeying all park traffic signs and regulations. Do not ride on sidewalks, trails, or fields.

- Do not climb on or disturb cannon, monuments, interpretive signs, or markers.

- Keep pets under physical control at all times. Pets are not allowed in buildings. If you must leave your pet unattended in a vehicle, remember to open window one to two inches for pet's safety and comfort.

- Individual public camping is not provided in the park. Organized youth group camping is permitted by reservation only.

- The possession or use of metal detectors in the park is prohibited. Artifact-hunting is not allowed.

- Picnic at designated areas only. These are located on South Confederate Avenue and at the rear of the Visitor Center. Fires are limited to propane, gasoline, and kerosene stoves.

- Watch for deer while traveling the park tour roads. Animals are especially numerous near roadways at dawn and dusk.

- Travel through the park on tour roads is limited to the period 6:00 A.M. to 10:00 P.M. daily.

- Contact a Park Ranger if you have questions about these or other regulations and activities.

SUMMARY OF CAMPAIGN

Background

The Civil War began on April 12, 1861, with the Confederate bombardment and capture of Fort Sumter in Charleston, South Carolina and continued for four years. The conflict that resulted in more than 600,000 casualties ended on April 9, 1865, when General Robert E. Lee surrendered to General Ulysses S. Grant at Appomattox Courthouse, Virginia. In the midst of this war, the turning point and bloodiest battle raged around the south-central Pennsylvania town of Gettysburg, July 1-2-3, 1863.

The Union Army of the Potomac, commanded by Major General George Gordon Meade, came to Gettysburg with approximately 97,000 men. This army was divided into seven infantry corps plus cavalry and artillery. Lieutenant General Robert Edward Lee commanded the Confederate Army of Northern Virginia in this battle. Lee's army, with an approximate strength of 75,000 men, was divided into three infantry corps plus cavalry and artillery.

The Battle in Brief

Confederate armies in the East had established an impressive list of victories by the Spring of 1863, but shortages in manpower and supplies shadowed their future. This situation led Confederate authorities to plan a northern invasion. They hoped that a successful campaign in Pennsylvania would net much needed supplies while Confederate forces lived off the land. They also hoped to draw the Union army out of exhausted Virginia; take the ravages of war north, in order to stimulate vocal northern peace advocates and gain foreign support. If successful, Lee intended to position his army to strike at Philadelphia, Baltimore, or Washington, thus increasing the possibility that Union authorities would be forced to accept a negotiated peace and southern independence.

On June 3, 1863, Lee began a march that carried his army west from their winter headquarters in Fredericksburg, Virginia, then north through the Shenandoah and Cumberland valleys. By the end of June, the main body of Lee's army was concentrated around Chambersburg, Pennsylvania with elements scattered as far as Carlisle, York, and the Harrisburg area. Confederate cavalry under General Jeb Stuart was far out of position at this time, and Lee was without essential reports on the advancing Federals.

The Union Army of the Potomac, under General Joseph Hooker, paralleled the Confederate advance north. Moving along the eastern side of the Blue Ridge Mountains, Hooker's forces remained between Lee's army and Washington, D.C. Command of the Union army changed during this march. Disagreements between Hooker and Union authorities led to Hooker's resignation. General George G. Meade, Hooker's Fifth Corps commander, assumed command and continued to move the army north.

Upon learning of the rapid advance of the Union army, Lee abandoned plans to move on Harrisburg and on June 28, ordered his troops to concentrate near Cashtown, eight miles west of Gettysburg. Meade established headquarters near Taneytown, Maryland on June 30 and ordered General John

Buford's cavalry division north to scout the Gettysburg area. As Buford's men approached, they were observed by Confederate infantry sent to Gettysburg in search of supplies. Without orders to bring on an engagement, General James Pettigrew's Confederate infantry brigade returned to Cashtown. Thus the opposing armies had accidentally set the stage for the Battle of Gettysburg.

This battle opened with a meeting of advanced elements of each army July 1, 1863. Starting about 8:00 A.M., fighting continued west of Gettysburg most of the morning. As additional troops arrived, the field of battle enlarged to include the plains area north of Gettysburg. Bitter engagements ensued to the west and north of town during much of the afternoon. In the face of superior Confederate field positions and troop strength, the Union army was forced to retreat through the town and regroup on Cemetery Hill and Culp's Hill to the south. Content with the day's actions, the Confederates did not follow up this initial victory.

Both Union flanks saw intense action on July 2. Confederate General James Longstreet's troops struck the left during the afternoon. In fierce fighting that lasted until dusk, his forces managed to break through an advanced line, but failed to take the Federal left. General Richard Ewell's attack on the Union right came during the evening. It too failed, but the Rebels did manage to establish a hold on a small portion of the southern slope of Culp's Hill around Spangler's Spring. The second day ended as a draw.

Fighting on July 3 began at dawn with a Union assault on positions around Spangler's Spring taken by Confederate troops the previous day. Fighting almost until noon, Federal troops regained this area. At 3:00 P.M., following a massive artillery barrage, General George Pickett began the final engagement of the battle. In less than an hour, Pickett's Charge, a massed infantry assault toward the Union center, was shattered. At this same time, Confederate cavalry moving toward the Union rear was intercepted by Northern cavalry, three miles east of town. The second and final Confederate invasion attempt had thus been halted. The bloodiest battle of the war, with some 51,000 casualties, was over.

Lee began retreating from Pennsylvania on the afternoon of July 4. As a result of Meade's hesitation to follow up his victory, Lee was able to move his army through Maryland and back into Virginia unmolested. Even after the serious defeat at Gettysburg, Lee continued the war for an additional twenty-two months.

McPherson Ridge

The white and fieldstone structure located on the McPherson Ridge today is the restored barn of the McPherson Farm for which the ridge is named. Located a mile west of Gettysburg, this ridge extends north from Reynolds' Woods, your present location, to Oak Hill.

The battle opened at about 8:00 A.M., July 1, 1863, when Confederate artillery and infantry struck General Buford's dismounted Union cavalry deployed along this ridge. Determined to hold and await reinforcements, Buford's men met initial assaults from the Confederate brigades of Archer and Davis. General John Reynolds' First Corps, arriving about 10:00 A.M., provided timely support for the embattled cavalrymen.

Shortly after his arrival on the field, Reynolds was killed. General Reynolds was the only corps commander killed during the battle.

Fighting continued along the reinforced Union line through the morning, with a lull coming about noon. At the end of the morning's action, the Confederates had been forced back to Herr Ridge, a mile to the west. Fighting began anew about 1:00 P.M. with the arrival of additional reinforcements for both sides. By the end of the day's action, Union troops were forced to retreat south of the town. Confederates overran their positions here on this ridge. Lee arrived from the west by way of the Chambersburg Pike, the road just ahead of you, in time to observe the Union retreat. He established headquarters along this road, just east of here. Three days later, Confederates again crossed this ridge as General John Imboden led a seventeen-mile long wagon train of dead and wounded Confederates out of Gettysburg.

The McPherson Barn on McPherson Ridge.

★ Eternal Light Peace Memorial

The Eternal Light Peace Memorial, dedicated on July 3, 1938, stands as a tribute to both Union and Confederate soldiers who fought at Gettysburg. This $60,000 monument was dedicated on the occasion of the 75th Anniversary of the battle. President Franklin D. Roosevelt was the principal speaker at ceremonies attended by more than 1800 Civil War veterans. The average age of these honored guests was 95.

Located on Oak Hill, northwest of Gettysburg, the Peace Light stands as a permanent reminder of the cherished goal of "Peace Eternal in a Nation United." With the exception of a brief interruption during World War II, a natural gas flame burned atop the monument from 1938 until 1974 when it was extinguished as an energy conservation measure. The high purpose of this memorial could not be ignored. In 1978, with the enthusiastic support of local citizenry, an energy-efficient electric lighting system was installed, restoring the "Eternal Light."

From this position, Confederate guns shelled Oak Ridge and the fields below. Infantry organized here and moved against the Union positions on Oak Ridge during the afternoon of July 1.

The Eternal Light Peace Memorial.

★ Oak Ridge

Rodes' Confederates, moving south from Carlisle, took the advantageous position of Oak Hill, a mile northwest of town. To meet the threat of Confederates arriving on Oak Hill, General Doubleday, Union First Corps commander following the death of Reynolds, deployed General John Robinson's division along this ridge. Oak Ridge lies between Oak Hill and McPherson Ridge. Tremendous engagements occurred along this line starting at 1:00 P.M. Two attacking Confederate brigades failed to dislodge Union troops from this position, but a third brigade, attacking from Oak Hill was successful. With the retreat of the Eleventh Corps from their line north of town and the resulting threat that Robinson's line of retreat may have been interrupted, Union positions here on Oak Hill were abandoned.

Oak Ridge from near the Mummasburg Road.

 ## North Carolina Memorial

Standing as a lasting tribute to the sons of North Carolina at Gettysburg, this memorial was dedicated in July, 1929. The five bronze figures represent a segment of Heth's Confederate division as they moved toward the Union positions on Cemetery Ridge as a part of Pickett's Charge. The sculptor, Gutzon Borglum, is best known for his tribute to four presidents on the face of Mount Rushmore in South Dakota.

The memorials from Virginia and North Carolina are situated near the center of the Confederate line along Seminary Ridge. This area served as the staging grounds for the three Confederate divisions involved in Pickett's Charge. After failing to breach the Union center, the battered Confederates returned to this line to await orders to begin their retreat from Gettysburg the following day. (A more detailed account of these actions is offered in the section entitled HIGH WATER MARK and VIRGINIA MEMORIAL.)

The North Carolina Memorial.

 Virginia Memorial

General Robert E. Lee, Confederate commander, and his favorite horse, Traveler, surmount the memorial from Virginia. The seven bronze figures at the base represent the various lifestyles of Virginians who rendered service during the war. The memorial was formally dedicated in 1917 by Virginia, Lee's native state. In 1987 the memorial was rededicated following extensive restoration efforts.

On July 3 Lee observed Pickett's Charge from this position along Seminary Ridge. Following their tragic failure, he rode out to rally his defeated and broken soldiers. Lee assumed full responsibility for the charge, the defeat at Gettysburg, and the failure of his second and final invasion of the North. Reflecting later, he commented, "Too bad! Too bad! Oh! Too bad!"

The Virginia Memorial.

Pitzer Woods

Opposing troops met here shortly after noon on July 2 and provided a grim prelude to the day's action on the Union left. The Third Maine Infantry and the Berdan Sharpshooters met massing Confederates as they prepared to strike Meade's left. Following a brief yet sharp encounter, this Union reconnaissance force recrossed the Emmitsburg Road and reported to General Sickles. With this information, Sickles decided to advance toward the Emmitsburg Road. (The line he formed is described in the section on Little Round Top.) About 4:00 P.M. Longstreet's assault on the Union left began. Confederate brigades moved west from the cover of Pitzer Woods to strike at Sickles' advanced positions.

Pitzer Woods and West Confederate Avenue.

Warfield Ridge

On the afternoon of July 2, soldiers of General Longstreet's I Corps began their attack against the Union left flank, from this ridge. This action began about 4:00 PM and marked the beginning of the second day of fighting. Longstreet's men engaged Union troops in the Devil's Den, the Wheatfield, the Peach Orchard, and on Little Round Top. By the conclusion of fighting on July 2, much of the area between this ridge and Little Round Top had changed hands numerous times, and casualty figures ran high on both sides. However, the day's action did not result in a victory for either army.

Warfield Ridge.

Little Round Top

Lee's strategy for the second day called for simultaneous attacks against both Union flanks. Longstreet's First Corps would hit the Union left while Ewell was to direct his Second Corps in an assault against Culp's Hill and Cemetery Hill on the Union right.

General Daniel Sickles, Union Third Corps commander, held Meade's left flank along the southern end of Cemetery Ridge just north of Little Round Top. At noon on July 2, Sickles sent a small reconnaissance force west to learn what was in front of him. Encountering Confederates in Pitzer Woods, this force retreated to report. Fearing that the Confederates may outflank him, Sickles began moving his corps west to what he felt was more advantageous ground. Without orders to do so, he formed a new line. With its left flank in Devil's Den, Sickles' line extended northwestward through the Wheatfield and on to the Peach Orchard where it extended northward along the Emmitsburg Road. In this forward position, Little Round Top was left virtually unoccupied.

Longstreet's troops began moving against Sickles' advanced line between 3:30 and 4:00 P.M. As engagements broke out along Sickles' line, General Evander Law's Alabama troops and Texas and Arkansas troops under General Jerome Robertson moved toward Little Round Top. Meade's chief engineer, General G. K. Warren, had made his way to the summit of Little Round Top and immediately recognized its significance. When he arrived, it was occupied only by men of the signal corps. Noting that it would be difficult to reposition Sickles' men, Warren sought aid from Fifth Corps troops moving toward the action in the Wheatfield. In response, Colonel Strong Vincent moved his brigade to the summit just in time to engage the advancing infantry of Law's Alabamians. Union General Stephen Weed's brigade fortified the western summit of Little Round Top as Robertson's Confederates pushed up that slope. Union artillery under Lieutenant Charles Hazlett moved their guns up the rocky eastern slope to take part in defending this location. Extremely heavy fighting continued for several hours, but in the end Little Round Top remained in Union hands. The defense of this position was costly to the Union army. Warren was wounded while Weed, Vincent, and Hazlett were killed. As a result of his timely action, General G. K. Warren won the nickname, "Savior of Little Round Top." Ewell delayed his attack on the Union right until late in the day. The failure to coordinate with Longstreet's assault on the left would prove significant to the outcome of the battle.

The summit of Little Round Top looking south.

The western slope of Little Round Top looking across the Valley of Death from Devil's Den.

The Wheatfield

This position was held by the Union Third Corps after General Sickles moved west from Cemetery Ridge. Sickles had moved his line shortly after noon on July 2. Intense fighting erupted here when the Confederate First Corps moved against the Union left later in the afternoon. To meet the advance of Longstreet's Confederates, troops from at least two additional Union corps became involved in and around the Wheatfield. During the wild and confused fighting, the field changed hands numerous times. By day's end, an estimated 6000 fallen Union and Confederate soldiers lay strewn across this trampled area. Both armies held positions around the Wheatfield until the end of the battle when the Confederates withdrew.

The Wheatfield looking toward the west.

⭐ The Peach Orchard

Action opened on July 2 with an intense duel between Union guns in the Peach Orchard and Confederate artillery positioned to the south and west. About 4:00 P.M., Hood's Confederate division crossed the Emmitsburg Road to meet Sickles' forward line. The Union line, in the shape of a "V," had its apex here in the Peach Orchard. Humphrey's brigade extended northward along the Emmitsburg Road toward Gettysburg, while Birney's brigade extended southeastward through the Wheatfield and the Devil's Den. In four hours of vigorous fighting, Sickles' line crumbled as Confederates overran the Peach Orchard. The Confederate success was costly, and at day's end Meade still retained his positions along Cemetery Ridge and Little Round Top. The timely and diligent service of Union reinforcements saved the Federal left.

Lee's July 3 artillery assault prior to Pickett's Charge began on a signal from two Confederate guns near here. In 1863 the Peach Orchard was much larger than it is today.

The Peach Orchard looking east toward Little Round Top in the distance.

During the action on July 2, advancing and retreating Union soldiers crossed and recrossed Plum Run several times. This run flows through a small valley that runs between Little Round Top on the east and the Wheatfield and the Devil's Den on the west. Since the battle, this valley has been known as the "Valley of Death." Some who witnessed the fighting along Plum Run reported that its waters had a tint of red, from the blood of soldiers killed and wounded along its banks. Because of these accounts, Plum Run is often referred to as "Bloody Run."

Plum Run in the Valley of Death.

★ Pennsylvania Memorial

Dedicated on September 27, 1910, at a cost of $150,000, this memorial stands on an 80 feet square base and rises to a height of 110 feet. Bronze tablets surrounding the base bear the names of the more than 34,500 Pennsylvanians involved in the battle. Pennsylvanians made up more than one-third of the Union forces at Gettysburg. Bronze figures around the center pay tribute to President Lincoln, Pennsylvania's Civil War governor, Andrew Curtin, and numerous Union officers from Pennsylvania. General George Gordon Meade, commander of the Army of the Potomac, is among the notable officers from Pennsylvania. The winged bronze figure atop the memorial represents the Goddess of Victory and Peace. The Pennsylvania Memorial is the largest of the more than 1300 memorials, markers, and tablets on the field. Following an extensive face lift, the memorial was rededicated in 1986.

The Pennsylvania Memorial.

★ Spangler's Spring

Located at the southern end of Culp's Hill, Spangler's Spring is named for its owner, Abraham Spangler. The cool water of this spring alternately refreshed the troops of both armies. Union troops held this valuable water supply until called to support other areas of their line during Longstreet's attack on the afternoon of July 2. During the evening of the second day's fighting, Johnson's Confederates took the spring and adjacent Union breastworks without a fight. The spring changed hands again on the morning of the final day of the battle, when Union troops returned and battled Johnson's men. Shortly before noon on July 3, Spangler's Spring was back in Union hands.

Spangler's Spring.

Cemetery Hill

The Evergreen Cemetery, Gettysburg's public cemetery since 1853, is situated along the southeastern slope and gives this hill its name. The survivors of the defeated Union First and Eleventh Corps struggled to regroup here late on the afternoon of July 1. General Lee observed their efforts and urged General Ewell to "press those people" from this advantageous position. Ewell did not push the defeated Union troops. Without opposition the weakened and vulnerable Union army reorganized and fortified their defenses south of town. Ewell's inaction proved costly, for the next day the same position proved to be an insurmountable obstacle.

Ewell's attack on Culp's Hill and Cemetery Hill was to take place in conjunction with Longstreet's move on the Union left. Ewell's artillery opened against Meade's right between 3:30 and 4:00 P.M. as planned, but his infantry attack toward these hills was delayed no less than three hours. Early's division assaulted and reached the crest of Cemetery Hill, engaging the Federal defenders in hand-to-hand combat. As darkness set in, desperate fighting continued. An attack against the western slope of Cemetery Hill never materialized. Because of this, Hancock was able to send reinforcements against Early's weakening troops. Unable to hold their ground, Early's men retreated around 10:00 P.M. Lee's attack against the Union right on the second day had failed.

Cemetery Hill from the south.

High Water Mark

Fighting on the second day doubtless served as an indication to Lee that Meade's line may have been weakest at its center along Cemetery Ridge. Assaults against the Union flanks had failed, but General Ambrose Wright's brigade of Georgians did manage to briefly pierce the Union line just south of the Copse of Trees. Against the advice of General Longstreet, Confederate First Corps commander, Lee planned to thrust at the Union center on July 3. He hoped to open the Federal position then capture or destroy the shattered units. This movement was the climax of the battle.

In an order to soften the Union center, some 140 Confederate cannon began bombarding that position at 1:00 P.M. More than 100 guns along Cemetery Ridge returned fire, resulting in a tremendous duel heard for miles. After about an hour and a half of constant firing, General Henry Hunt, Union artillery chief, ordered his guns to cease firing to conserve ammunition and allow the guns to cool. Confederate First Corps artillery commander, Colonel E. P. Alexander, observing this duel from the Peach Orchard, interpreted Hunt's action to mean that Union guns had been silenced. He ordered Pickett to begin the advance toward Cemetery Ridge.

Pickett's Charge, as the final act of the battle is known, began about 3:00 P.M. General George Pickett's division, along with divisions led by Generals Pettigrew and Trimble, moved from Seminary Ridge still partially screened by smoke from the artillery duel. Union infantry and artillery lay in wait. Union fire opened on the Confederate divisions, numbering about 12,000, as they crossed the Emmitsburg Road. Double-canister artillery and withering infantry volleys cut gaping holes, but the gray line pressed forward toward the Copse of Trees, their objective. General Winfield Hancock's Second Corps, holding the center of the Union line, faced the charging Confederates.

By the time the Confederates reached the stone wall, all order disappeared and the line crumbled. Vermont regiments of General George Stannard's brigade struck the right flank of the Confederate line while the left crumbled under Union crossfire and retreated in disorganization. In a daring effort at the center, General Lewis Armistead and 150 men crossed the stone wall and entered the area of the Angle only to be killed, wounded, or captured. The time that elapsed during Pickett's Charge was less than an hour. During that time, two-thirds of the attacking Confederates fell or were taken captive.

The High Water Mark looking toward the southwest. Copse of trees and General Meade statue at left.

The High Water Mark.

National Cemetery

Fighting ended in Gettysburg on July 3, but the horrors of war remained. Pennsylvania governor, Andrew Curtin, visited the town a few days after the battle. The need for proper burial grounds was obvious, so the Governor appointed David Wills, a local attorney, to select a site and organize a cemetery. Before the end of August, Wills had chosen and purchased a 17 acre plot on Cemetery Hill. William Saunders, a noted landscape architect, was selected to design the cemetery.

Ceremonies to dedicate the grounds took place on November 19, 1863. The principal speaker was Edward Everett, President of Harvard University. A noted orator of the day, Everett spoke for almost two hours. President Lincoln had also been asked to deliver "a few appropriate remarks" at the dedication. Lincoln's "Gettysburg Address," one of the most noted orations in human history, was delivered in a little over two minutes. Lincoln was not impressed with his speech. Time, however, has rendered a different verdict. Monuments to Lincoln and his address stand at the south end of the cemetery and at the center of the Civil War plots. The Soldiers' National Monument, to your left, was dedicated in 1869 as the first memorial in Gettysburg. It stands on the spot where Lincoln stood to speak. The Genius of Liberty stands atop this memorial with figures representing War, Peace, Plenty, and History around the base.

Union soldiers numbering more than 3,500 rest permanently in this cemetery. Of that number, about half are unknown. No Confederate soldiers are known to have been buried here. In the years since the Civil War, the bodies of American servicemen from all succeeding conflicts have been added.

An early, post-Civil War view of the Gettysburg National Cemetery (GNMP).

The Soldiers' National Memorial in the National Cemetery.

Abraham Lincoln photographed in November 1863 (USAMHI).

Cemetery dedication parade on Baltimore Street, November 19, 1863 (USAMHI).

Cemetery dedication ceremonies, November 19, 1863 (GNMP).

Today five autographed copies of the Gettysburg Address are known to exist. The first two copies were written in 1863. They are known as the Nicolay and Hay copies, because they were given by Lincoln to his personal secretaries, Nicolay and Hay. These copies are now in the hands of the Library of Congress. Three additional copies were completed by Lincoln in 1864. These final three copies were given to Edward Everett, George Bancroft, and Alexander Bliss. The 1864 copies were to be sold for the benefit of the United States Sanitary Commission. Today the Everett copy is the property of the Illinois State Historical Library, the Bancroft copy is at Cornell University and the Bliss copy hangs in the Lincoln Room of the White House. During the summer a copy of the address is on display in the Cyclorama of the National Park Service.

July 1863 view of Culp's Hill taken from the Baltimore Pike on Cemetery Hill (GNMP).

OTHER POINTS OF INTEREST

Barlow Knoll

Barlow Knoll marked the right of the Union Eleventh Corps north of Gettysburg. General Oliver Howard's troops arrived in Gettysburg about noon on July 1 and formed a line between this knoll and the Mummasburg Road. General Francis Barlow's division held the knoll, and it is in his honor that it has been named. Howard's line withstood an attack by Confederates moving in from the north early in the afternoon. Jubal Early's Confederate division arrived from the north, greatly intensified action along Howard's position, and ultimately broke it. Early's troops formed the right of the 28,000 man Confederate arc north and west of town.

It soon became apparent that Howard's exposed line could not hold against flank and frontal assaults. After a gallant stand, the Eleventh Corps was compelled to retreat through the streets of Gettysburg. Disorganization marked this retreat and resulted in additional Union losses. With the fall of this line, Early was free to strike at the rear of the Union First Corps west of town; so they too retreated. By 5:00 P.M. the defeated Union army was regrouping on the hills south of town. Union losses for the first day were approximately two-thirds of the 18,000 involved.

Barlow Knoll.

Devil's Den

Devil's Den is the name given to the cluster of boulders on the west side of the Valley of Death. It marked the left flank of the ill-fated line established by Union General Sickles on July 2. While in Union hands, General Ward's brigade and Smith's New York artillery battery held the position. Union control of this area was brief. Shortly after Confederate troops opened the second day's fighting against the Union left, Hood's Confederate division gained control of Devil's Den. Confederate sharpshooters then positioned themselves among the huge rocks. These sharpshooters were responsible for numerous Union casualties on Little Round Top. Union artillery on Little Round Top shelled the area, inflicting heavy casualties, but the Confederates retained possession until the close of the battle.

Devil's Den.

Culp's Hill

Located on the Henry Culp farm southeast of town, Culp's Hill was one of the locations to which Union troops retreated following their defeat on July 1. It later marked the right flank of the Union defense positions. Following Lee's plan for coordinated attacks, Culp's Hill was bombarded with artillery as Longstreet's men began their drive against the Union left on the afternoon of July 2. Return fire from Union guns on Cemetery Hill quickly stifled the Confederate cannon. For reasons never fully explained, infantry assaults against this position were delayed until evening, by which time Longstreet's attack on the Union left had been stopped.

Johnson's brigade attacked Culp's Hill on the evening of the second day. His right surged gallantly toward the summit only to be reversed. His left, however, found very thinly manned Union breastworks and took them with virtually no resistance. Unaware of the fact that Union supply wagons were on the Baltimore Pike, a few hundred yards in front of him, and the generally weak condition of Union defenses in the area, Johnson did not press this advance. A tremendous opportunity was thus allowed to pass. Before dawn on the final day, Union troops returned in strength, and in fierce fighting that lasted about seven hours, regained their lost positions.

Culp's Hill area.

GETTYSBURG NOTES

The Battle of Gettysburg was the only major battle of the Civil War fought on Union soil. The 56th Pennsylvania Infantry Regiment fired the first infantry volley against the advancing Confederates on July 1.

Gettysburg is remembered as the "turning-point battle" of the Civil War, it was the "bloodiest battle" of the war, and it produced 62 Congressional Medal of Honor winners.

In all, 164,000 men made up the two armies at Gettysburg. There were 94,000 men in the Union Army of the Potomac, and there were 70,000 men in the Confederate Army of Northern Virginia.

On the first day of the battle, 27,000 Confederates and 20,000 Federals took part. During the second day, 34,000 Confederates battled 33,000 Union soldiers, and on July 3, approximately 20,000 soldiers took part for each army.

In all there were 46,000 casualties during the three days of fighting. There were 23,000 Confederate casualties (more than 32% of their total strength), and there were 23,000 Union casualties (less than 25% of their total strength). Of the 46,000 casualties, 8,000 were killed, 27,000 were wounded and 11,000 were listed as missing or captured.

The two armies that met in Gettysburg brought about 90,000 horses and mules with them. By the close of the fighting, more than 5,000 of these animals had been killed. The 9th Massachusetts Artillery Battery, (posted east of the Peach Orchard and later near the Trostle Farm), lost 80 of their 88 horses in this battle.

There were 626 pieces of artillery in Gettysburg during the battle. The Union army had 354 pieces, and the Confederate army had the remaining 272 pieces. Throughout the battle, it is estimated that there was 569 tons of artillery shells fired by the opposing armies.

In 1863 there were 2,400 residents living in Gettysburg. During the battle, only one civilian of Gettysburg was killed, and only one civilian was wounded. Mary Virginia "Jennie" Wade was killed on the morning of July 3. She was accidentally shot while baking in her sister's house on the northwestern slope of Cemetery Hill. John Burns, the only Gettysburg civilian known to have taken part in the battle, fought alongside the men of the 150th Pennsylvania Infantry, during the action on the morning of July 1, along McPherson Ridge. Burns was wounded three times, but survived and became known as the "civilian hero" of the battle.

Samuel Wilkeson, a war reporter for the *New York Times,* filed an excellent account of the Union defeat on July 1. As a part of his story he

July 1863 view of the Trostle Farm (USAMHI).

July 1863 view of the Evergreen Cemetery Gate House (GNMP).

reported the death of a 19-year-old Union artillery commander, killed in action north of the town. The young artillery commander, Bayard Wilkeson, was the son of the *New York Times* reporter.

Wesley Culp was killed in Gettysburg on his uncle's farm. This Confederate soldier is believed to be buried in an unmarked plot on Culp's Hill. William, Wesley's brother, also served during the Civil War, but in a Union uniform.

A strange friendship was born between opposing generals on the afternoon of July 1. Confederate General J.B. Gordon stopped on what is now Barlow Knoll to give aid to Union General Francis Barlow. By the end of the war misinformation led both men to believe the other to be dead. Several years after the war, they renewed their friendship, after meeting at a dinner given by a mutual friend. They remained close friends until Barlow's death.

General George Pickett graduated from the United States Military Academy at West Point in the class of 1846. His appointment to the academy was signed by Illinois Congressman Abraham Lincoln. There were 59 graduates in the class of 1846—Pickett's rank was 59.

Union General Daniel Sickles, the Third Corps commander, was a Congressman from New York. Confederate General William Barksdale, a brigade commander in Longstreet's First Corps, was a Congressman from Mississippi. Both men were wounded in action on July 2. Barksdale died the following day. Sickles had to have a leg amputated. Rather than having it disposed of, Sickles ordered that it be preserved and made into a "trophy." Today, the bones of that "trophy" are still on display at the Walter Reed Medical Museum in Washington, DC.

Lieutenant Henry Wentz commanded a Confederate artillery battery near the Peach Orchard. This position was familiar to young Wentz, because his guns were posted in the yard of his boyhood home. Although Wentz had moved south some years before the war, his family still lived in Gettysburg.

World War II General George S. Patton's great-uncle, Colonel W.T. Patton was attached to the 7th Virginia Infantry Regiment.

Father William Corby was the chaplain of the famous Irish Brigade of the Union army. After the war, Father Corby became the president of Notre Dame University.

Confederate General James A. Walker (Johnson's Division of the II Corps) had been dismissed from the Virginia Military Institute, because he challenged a professor, T. J. "Stonewall" Jackson, to a duel. At Gettysburg, Walker commanded Jackson's "Stonewall" Brigade. Walker was later granted his diploma for distinguished service to the Confederacy.

Union casualties at Gettysburg (USAMHI).

Confederate prisoners on Seminary Ridge (USAMHI).

When fighting broke out between the North and the South in 1861, a Union command position was offered to General Robert E. Lee, a distinguished American soldier. Between 1852 and 1855 General Lee had been the superintendent of the United States Military Academy at West Point. Unable to take up arms against his native state of Virginia, Lee cast his lot with the Confederacy. To this day, Lee remains one of America's most honored military figures.

General Joseph R. Davis commanded Confederate troops during the battle. His uncle was the Confederate President, Jefferson Davis.

Union troops under General Reynolds' command, and Confederate troops under General Archer's command opposed each other on the morning of July 1. Both generals were casualties of this action. Reynolds was killed just 15 minutes after he arrived on the field and was the only corps commander killed in the battle. Archer was taken prisoner when his brigade hit the Union Iron Brigade. General Archer was the first Confederate general taken prisoner since Lee assumed command of the Army of Northern Virginia in 1862.

The slopes of Culp's Hill are marked with monuments from four Maryland regiments: three Union regiments and one Confederate.

The flag of the 16th Maine Infantry Regiment was destroyed during the Union retreat on July 1. It was torn into little pieces by the men of the regiment, to prevent its capture by the enemy. Earlier in the day, they had lost the flag of Maine and the Stars and Stripes to the Confederates.

The flag of the 149th New York Volunteers gives a vivid indication of the fighting on Culp's Hill. There were 81 holes in the flag and seven in the staff of the flag.

A sign on the gatehouse of the Evergreen Cemetery, at the time of the battle, stated that firearms were prohibited in the area.

On the afternoon of July 2, the 1st Minnesota Regiment went into battle with 262 men. By the close of the day, 215 of those men were killed or wounded. The 1st Minnesota suffered a loss of 82%, more than any other unit involved in the battle.

In 1913, an estimated 55,000 veterans of the Civil War visited Gettysburg during the 50th Anniversary of the battle. In 1938 there was an estimated 8,000 veterans still alive. Of that number, about 1,800 visited Gettysburg during the 75th Anniversary. There average age was 94.

The 151st Pennsylvania Infantry Regiment enlisted for service in 1862. Of the 900 members of the regiment, 113 were school teachers.

July 1863 view of the Valley of Death looking southeast toward Little Round Top (left) and Big Round Top (right) (USAMHI).

July 1863 view looking east from McPherson Ridge toward Reynolds Woods (right) and Seminary Ridge in the distance (USAMHI).

SUGGESTED READING LIST

"Gettysburg." *Civil War Times Illustrated,* Harrisburg, Pennsylvania: Historical Times, Inc., 1968.

Coddington, Edwin B. *The Gettysburg Campaign.* Dayton, Ohio: Morningside Bookshop, 1968.

Frassanito, William A. *Gettysburg: A Journey in Time.* New York, New York: Charles Scribner's Sons, 1975.

Stackpole, Edward J. *They Met At Gettysburg.* Harrisburg, Pennsylvania: Stackpole Books, 1956.

Storrick, William C. *The Battle of Gettysburg.* Gettysburg, Pennsylvania: Greenwood Horne Publishing Company, 1980.

Tilberg, Frederick. *Gettysburg.* Washington, DC: Government Printing Office, 1962.

Tucker, Glenn. *High Tide At Gettysburg.* Dayton, Ohio: Morningside Bookshop, 1973.

Young, Jesse Bowman. *The Battle of Gettysburg.* Dayton, Ohio: Morningside Bookshop, 1976.